CREATIVITREE

DESIGN IDEAS FOR FAMILY TREES

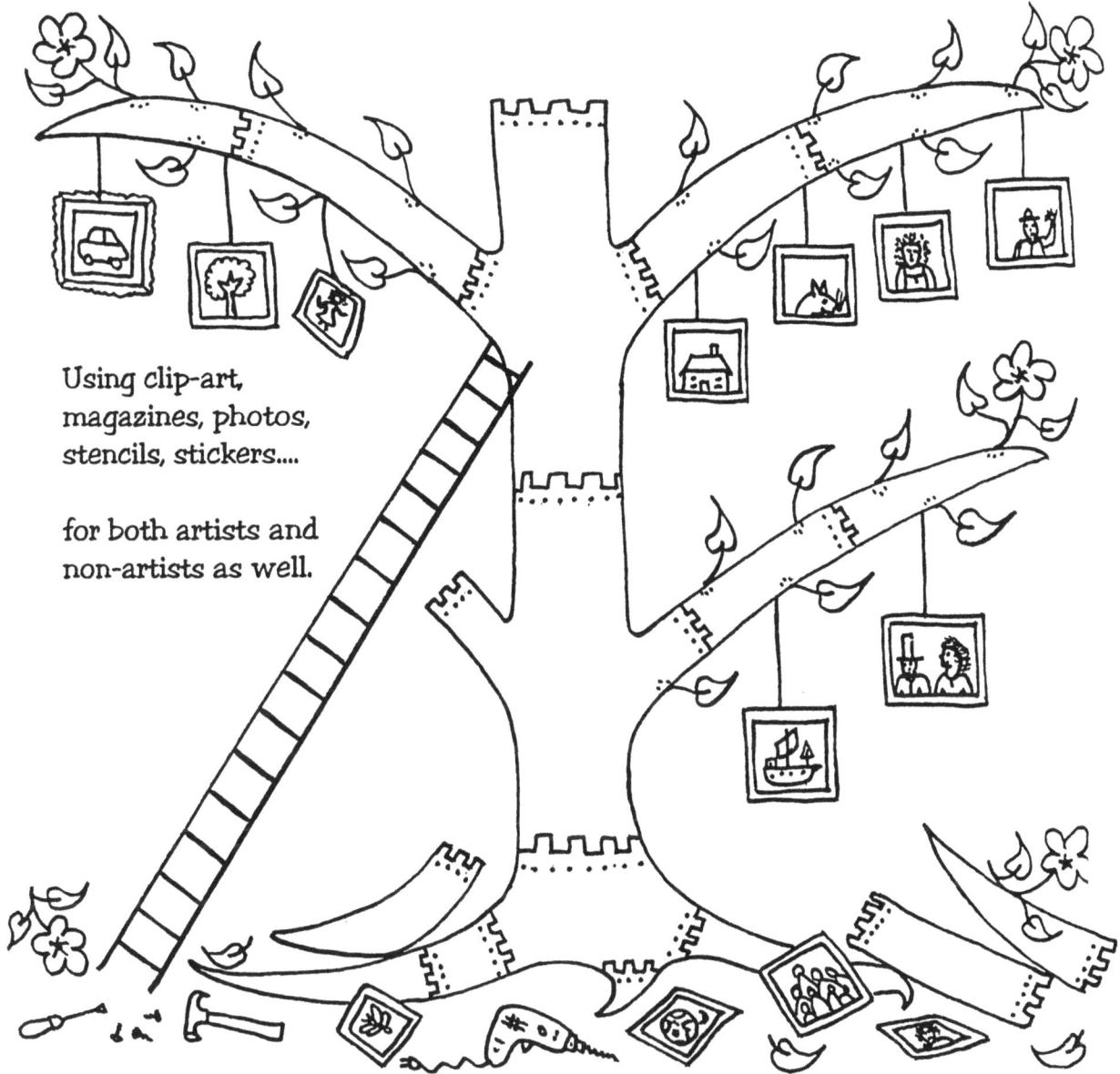

Using clip-art,
magazines, photos,
stencils, stickers....

for both artists and
non-artists as well.

TONY MATTHEWS

CLEARFIELD

Printed for
Clearfield Company, Inc. by
Genealogical Publishing Co., Inc.
Baltimore, Maryland
2001

International Standard Book Number: 0-8063-5118-7

Made in the United States of America

CREATIVITREE

by Tony Matthews

for Linda
for suggestions and support
along this different road

WELCOME..........

This should be fun, as I continue the family tree revolution that I began with my previous book, Paper Trees. This time, though, not only will I illustrate some aspects of that evolution, but will also show ways that you can easily create a beautiful, colourful, historic, humourous, or individual tree yourself, whether you are an artist or not.

THEORIES

First the important theories that this is all based upon :

1) Genealogy isn't just dusty books and muddy graveyards, it is a human thing, and thus open to colour, beauty, fun, imagination....

2) Likewise, family trees are about people, your people, and can be very individual, as well as open to colour, beauty, fun, imagination........

3) This is the one giant leap of creativitree.... a family tree doesn't have to actually look like a tree !

Once you absorb the theories, and see the examples that I'll use, I think that your creative juices will begin to flow. In fact, with all of the aids available, you don't even have to be artistic to achieve a good result. I spent many years as a gardener, and with this book I am simply hoping to plant some seeds. I would love to see what flowers YOU grow.

A family tree is made up of several elements. Most important are your ancestors' names, which you want to present clearly, in an organised way, and in a setting that creates interest and encourages its own preservation. You will have records of aunts, cousins, in-laws etc., that you keep in a shoe box under the bed....probably several shoe boxes, but I will mainly concentrate on the pedigree tree that is common to us all, namely 2 parents, 4 grandparents, 8 great grandparents, and so on.

There is some simple mathematics to help organise these names into a coherent design, and I will not only show you how it is done, but also include some blanks so that you can bypass this stage. Graph paper is great to work on, to keep it all symetrical and equally sized..... and the lines on graph paper don't reproduce on a copier.

Then we come to the pretty parts......or serious. A tree, like people, can also be formal. You don't even have to be an artist with so much clip art, computer designs, stencils, pictures in magazines, etc., available.

You can, of course, take a cue from my ideas, but the one thing that it is good to have is a simple theme, some concept, something that sets you and/or your family apart. There are also some obvious historical images that would be entirely suitable for a family tree. But I like to be different, and I hope that you do too. So, do you have a hobby, a career, a collection, a family business, a favourite something to use as your theme ? As an English gardener you won't be surprised to see flowers and castles appear on my designs, but are your family sailors or truckers, do you like dinosaurs or collect china pigs, are you into fashion or antique tools ? Any interest can be utilised on one or more of the different basic types of trees you'll discover in this book.

SQUARE ONE

But let's jump feet first into the middle of the revolution, for here we find one of the most versatile designs. On the next pages you will see Our World, and then the blank that it was based on, simply created with graph paper, pen and ruler. Consider that empty border, it is an open invitation to you to fill it with any images that you like ! Freedom !

Where to get these images ? I had a go at drawing them, but you can use clip-art, which is widely available in books and cds; photographs; pictures copied or cut from magazines, stencils, stickers, or any of the techniques that your local arts and craft shop will offer for use in scrap books, memory or photo albums........ Anyway, get some pictures, paste them on your blank tastefully, run a copy, and you are well on the way.

What images ? Family photos would be great, relevant scenery, houses, anything historical, fashions or jobs through the Ages, your favourite flowers, sports stars, clips from films, photos of those china pigs, ships, musical instruments, or whatever your particular theme is. The border is blank, there is no limit to what you put in it. Ask the family for suggestions. You may get so many ideas that either they will have a go themselves, or you will know what to do for their next birthday or Xmas present. Children might have fun cutting and pasting pictures on a border if you do the names, or let *them* write in the names......a perfect learning opportunity. Anything that creates interest is a help towards preserving your family history.

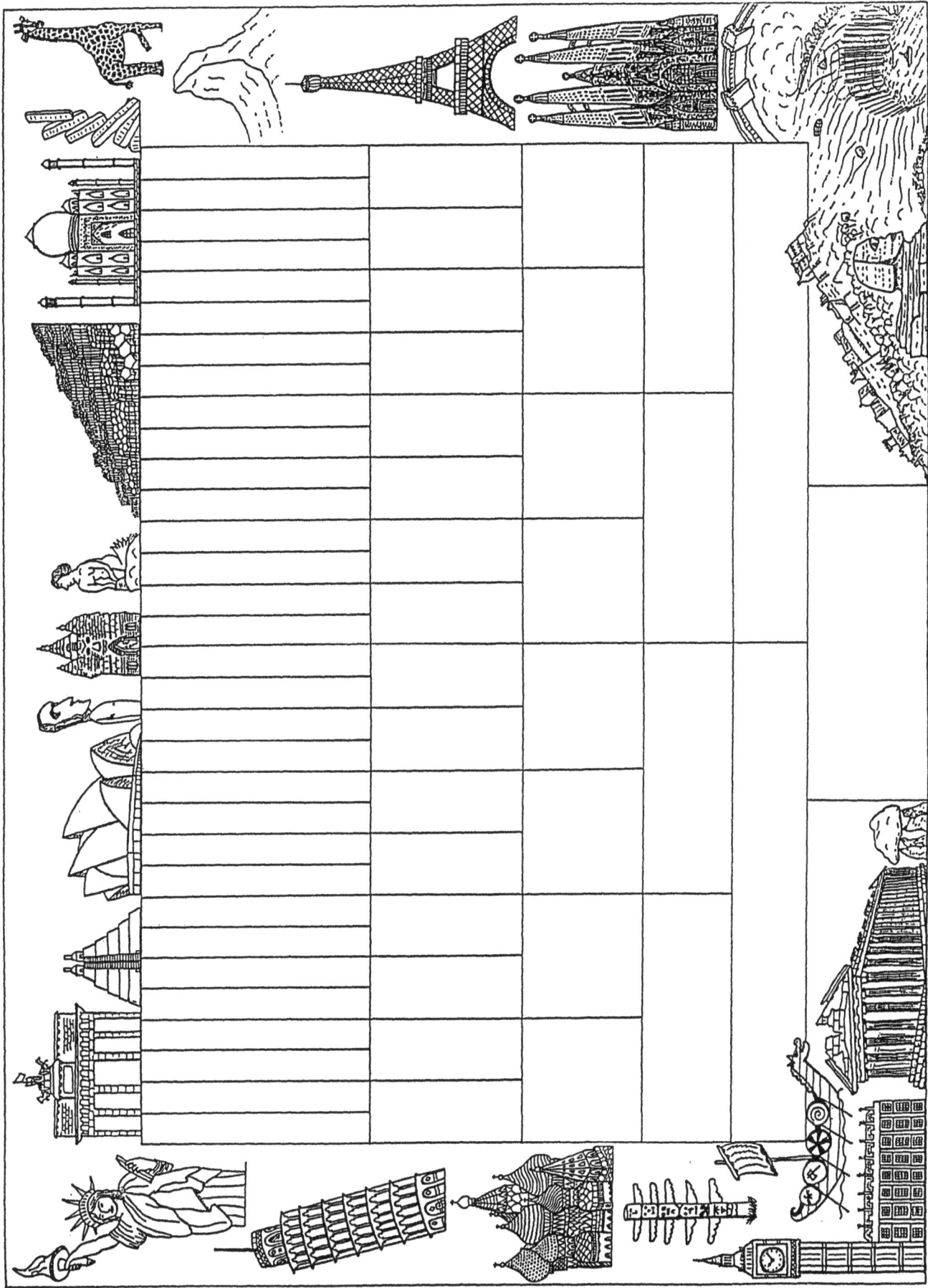

SPACED BOXES

Meanwhile, we will take our blank, and evolve it. What if we shrink those boxes a little, until there are spaces between them ? Now we have something different to work with. You could use a poster, wrapping paper, even pretty wallpaper. Then with a graph ruler, or light box with a grid on it (copy shops have them) paste on rectangles of coloured paper to match the picture, all straight and nicely spaced.

With plain paper you might use geometric or other designs to fill the spaces. Triangles or circles would be easy to colour in, but how about hearts, stars, dolphins or dinosaurs ? Check out school suppliers, they will have stencils to help you, or even stickers for the instant effect !

But my middle name should be Rose......I use them on many Trees, and they are in fact quite easy to draw. Not the full proper botanical version, of course, but what you might call a "design" . Several of the following have featured on my Trees, and there are some simple ones that I think most folk could do. Have a try.

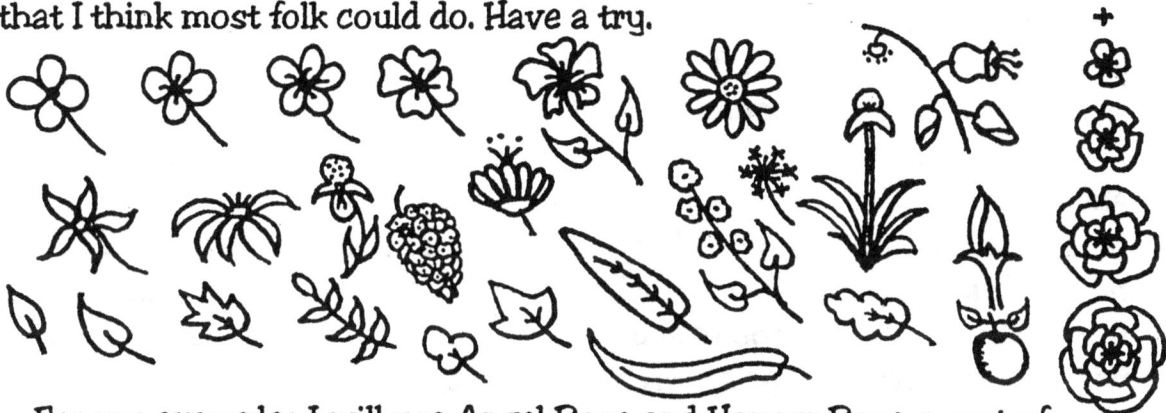

For my examples I will use Angel Rose and Honour Rose, a sort of "his 'n' hers". They look great framed and hanging side by side on the wall, but then if you get divorced you can each take yours with you !

I will include a blank that you just need to add a picture to. You could use anything else that is appropriate to you: your photo, your favourite car, house, landscape, a Space Station, or even something written, a poem or biblical tract. Use graph paper to draw your own squares (you can play with different sizes, to fit the page), then add shapes between them, maybe with clip-art or stencils, or hand-drawn (descendants would love that). The possibilities are endless, and, believe me, it would be hard NOT to create a decent tree. Again, you could put on a border. even those strips to match the wallpaper, maybe fabric, stencilled shapes, stickers......

FILLING IN

Before we get into more basic tree shapes, let's look at paper, pens, and how to fill in your tree, and what to do with it when it is finished, apart from framing and hanging it on your wall for all to admire.

First of all you want paper that is acid - free. Much of it is, nowadays, and copy shops, arts and craft stores, printers and paper suppliers, and even office suppliers carry some. It will last much longer than ordinary paper, and not turn so brown like, say, newspapers do. You may want to explore different sizes, colour, and texture. When you are copying your tree, or the pictures to go on it, a good copy shop can offer you different colours of print, not just the good old black and white. Of course they will do full colour copies of your work, or of the pictures or photos that you want to use.

Acid-free/archival pens are readily available now, too, not only for caligraphy, but in roller ball and other familiar types, with different sizes of nibs, and costing no more than an ordinary pen. Colours are a little more expensive, but getting cheaper.

The most common comment I get is " I couldn't fill one of those in, my handwriting's awful.". Well, mine is pretty awful too, but there are always alternatives. First, though, I must say that you are creating a family heirloom, and, if you sign and date it, a historical document. In a hundred years, think what a thrill for someone to find it, (in a dusty frame, leaning against the wall in the loft, behind the antique computer) with " great grandma/pa's own handwriting " on it.

So, how is your printing ? Most of us learnt it at school, and can do it perfectly well enough to be legible. I always advise you to do it lightly in pencil first, until it looks good. Then, the next day, you can check that you haven't got your grandfathers married to each other, and then ink over the pencil. Finally lightly erase any pencil still showing.

Not confident for even printing ? Has someone else in the family got a good hand ? Just as valuable to future generations. You could pay a calligrapher, but get permission to do copies of the finished Tree.

By the way, what is best to include, apart from the names ? I would suggest date and place of birth are most important, then date and place of marriage. If you have room you might add a distinguishing fact such as "carpenter". "bred black roses". "navy 1812 war", "great cook", or whatever..... it is your tree.

ROSE OF HONOUR

© Tony Matthews, 1999

Paper Tree Collections

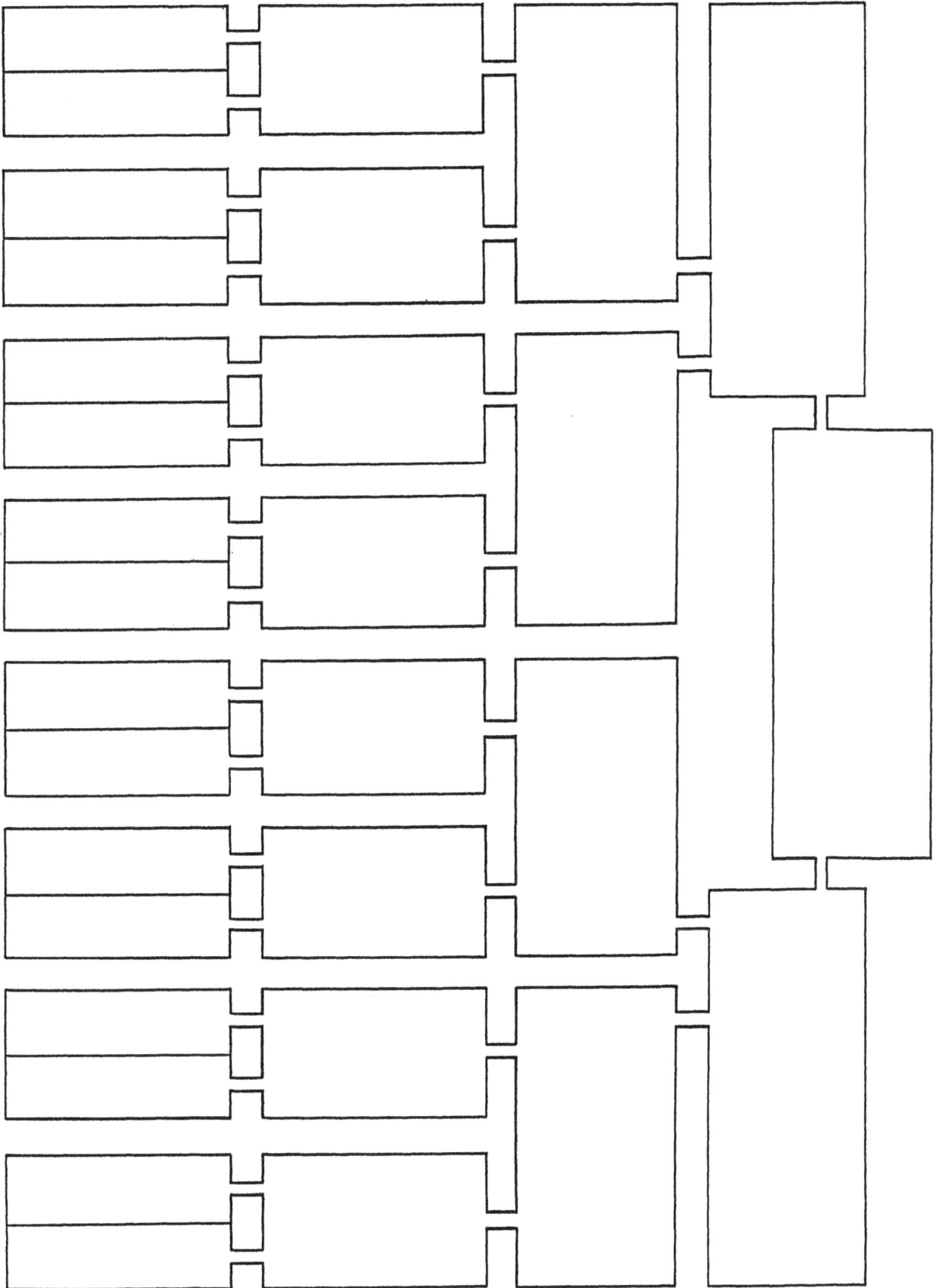

Then there is the machine method. You type your names in a nice font on a typewriter or computer. If you have neither, a good copy shop will, or a friend who works in an office, etc. Then you cut out the names and paste them onto your tree, and run off a really smart looking copy. You can do this on your blank, then add your pictures, or on the decorated version before having a copy made. Either way I always recommend making copies, and passing them on to other family members just for safe keeping, along with a copy of all of your validated info., photos, family tales, documents etc. I hear too many horror stories about whole uncopied collections being lost or destroyed.

But we are not content with just a pretty tree to hang on our wall, are we ? We can now store and display it in different ways. Copy it. Share it with family members. Photograph it. Add it to your photo cd. Scan it into your computer, add it to your webpage, email it all over the world, submit it to the LDS, your local library, or any library or genealogical society where you or your ancestors have called home.

We are not finished yet. Back to the copy shop (I must buy shares in them !) and you can soon be walking around with your tree printed on your t-shirt, drinking out of a mug with it on, carrying your genealogical books in a tote bag decorated with it.....you get the idea ? Then there's the family history book that you are writing, or the dividers in your family files. How about decorated blanks to pass out at the Reunion, for each group to fill in ? Oh, and did anyone mention genealogical Christmas cards ? You could both save money and make really good Christmas/Wedding/Birthday/Moving/ Get Well/ Halloween/ Anniversary/etc. presents.   I did a whole book full of them (Greetings) with messages and borders to mix 'n' match, then colour. Trees can be scanned into a computer, and coloured. You may have more ideas.... let me know ! I will include one Xmas card to whet your appetite. Many folk hang on to greetings cards, so here is another way to aid preservation of basic information. If any of my grandparents had given me even a 4 generation Tree, it would have saved me hours of research, some still ongoing. That was their only fault, though.

Without getting morbid, do a Tree today. Who knows what will happen tomorrow. Don't worry that you haven't "finished" your research......you never will.....and you can always add to your Tree as you go along, or do another, or other folk can continue it.

LET'S GET CURVY

Let's change shape now, and get curvy (the world is divided into square and curvy people, plus a few weirdos). On the next pages are examples which follow the same pattern as the previous square ones, but now fan shaped (or circular) with curved boxes, and curved boxes with spaces between them. You could also add a border as in the previous examples. This could relate to your theme, or be purely decorative. Try doing a simple one yourself, or there are some wonderfully ornate ones available as clip-art.

I have woven roses through one fan shape, but, again, clip art, stencils etc. could be used. Pictures could be just pasted around the fan or circle, or the fan/circle could be pasted onto a picture. Think laterally !

What things can you think of that are circular or semi-circular ? A clock face....a wheel.....a hill.......the door of a washing machine........a spider's web.........a peacock's tail......a fan.....a hot air balloon.......a turtle's shell.......keep thinking. Your circle/fan could be integral to the picture, or be framed by your additions, or have stuff woven in the spaces, or any combination.

I will include some blanks for your to copy and play with. Don't be afraid to make several copies of different sizes, scribble on ideas, then throw them away.....copies are cheap !

As before, you can fill in your Tree by hand, or cut 'n' paste printed names from a computer or typewriter. Most art programs allow you to do words in a curved shape.

Perhaps a 3 quarter circle would work for you ? Perhaps you could do arcs, but put regular rectangles in them, which might be easier to fill in ? This suggests an inverted V shape, like a pyramid........one idea can often spark off others. The circle could likewise become a diamond.

You can even open up your design a little more : you have 2 parents, and could halve the design, or even quarter it from your 4 grandparents. I used these concepts to create a butterfly's wings, and an elephant's ears. Quilters might see a design with you and your parents in the centre, and grandparents, with their parents, etc., as the cornerpieces.

I did several fans, with different numbers of generations, and had roses and other flowers climbing over them. It was interesting to take several of the same design, then colour them differently. This seemed to really change the whole look. Try it ?

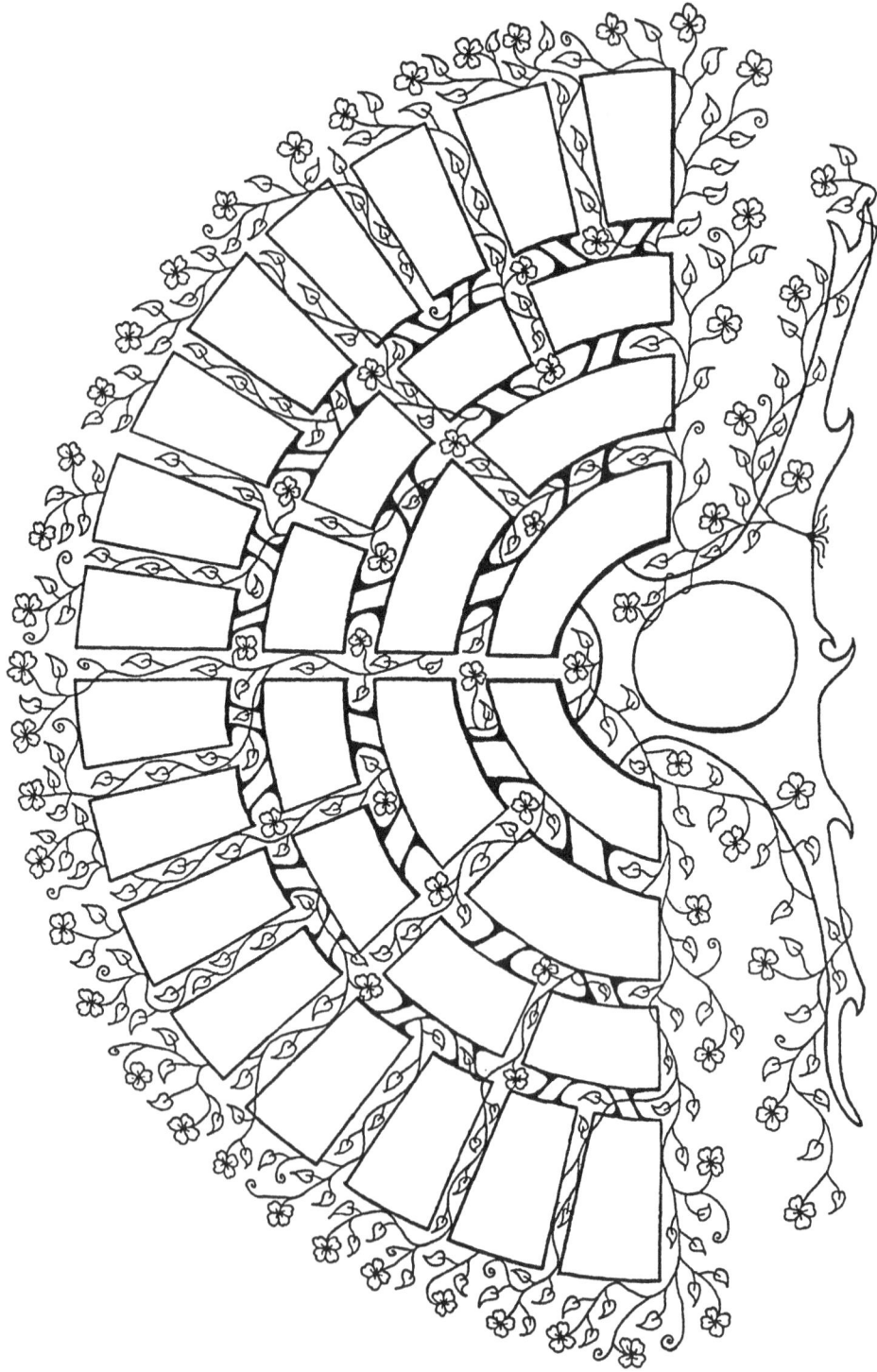

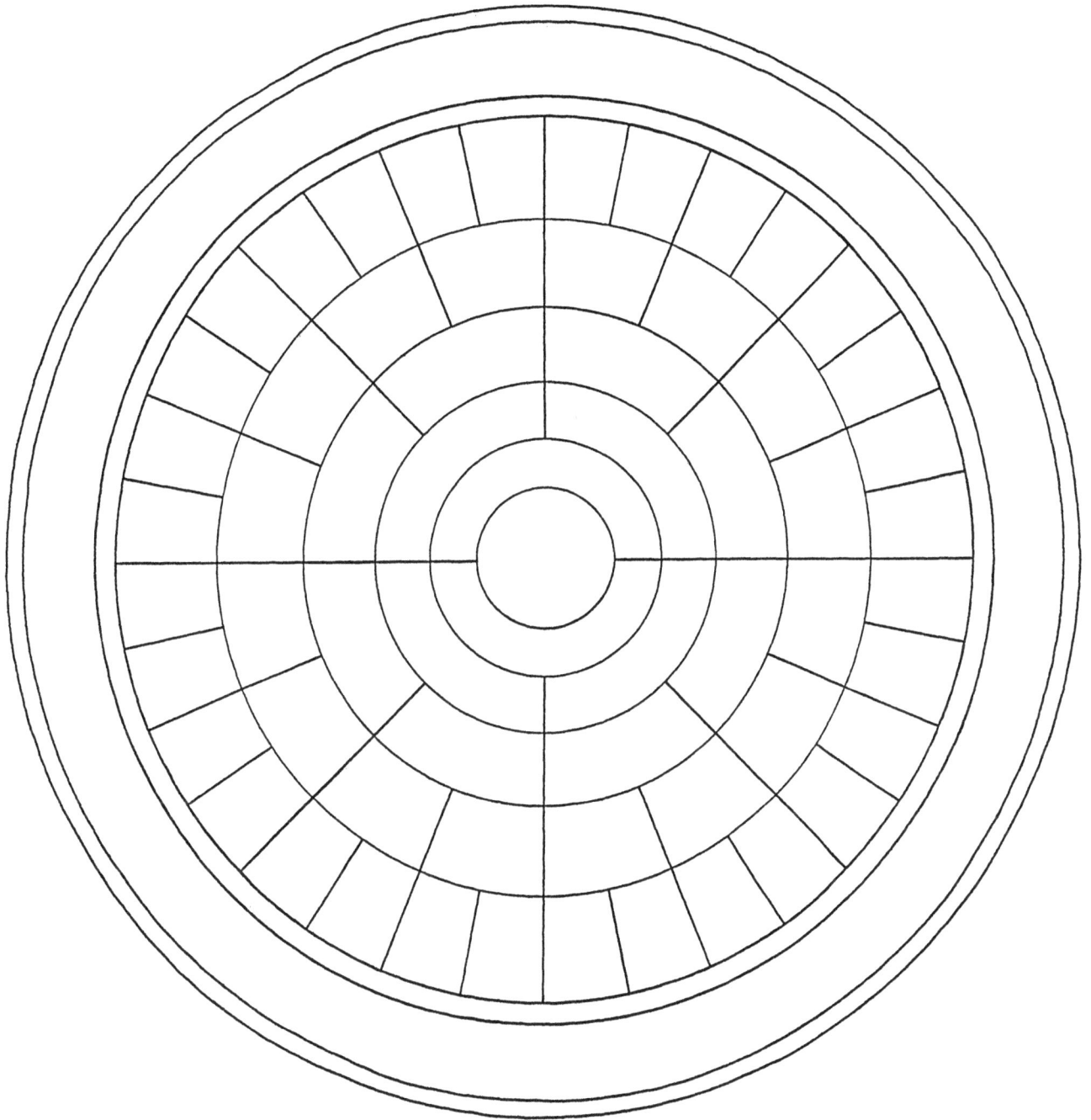

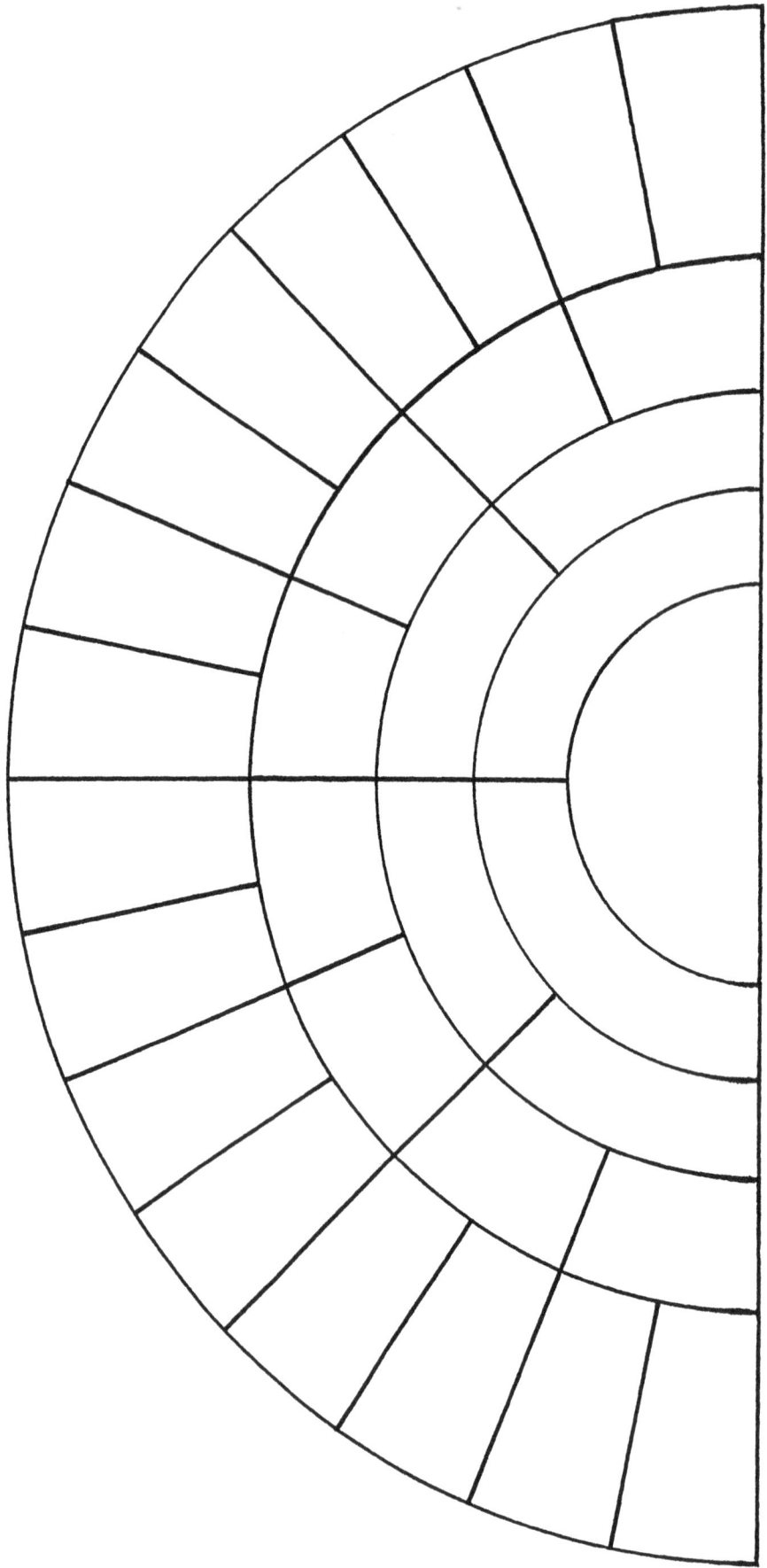

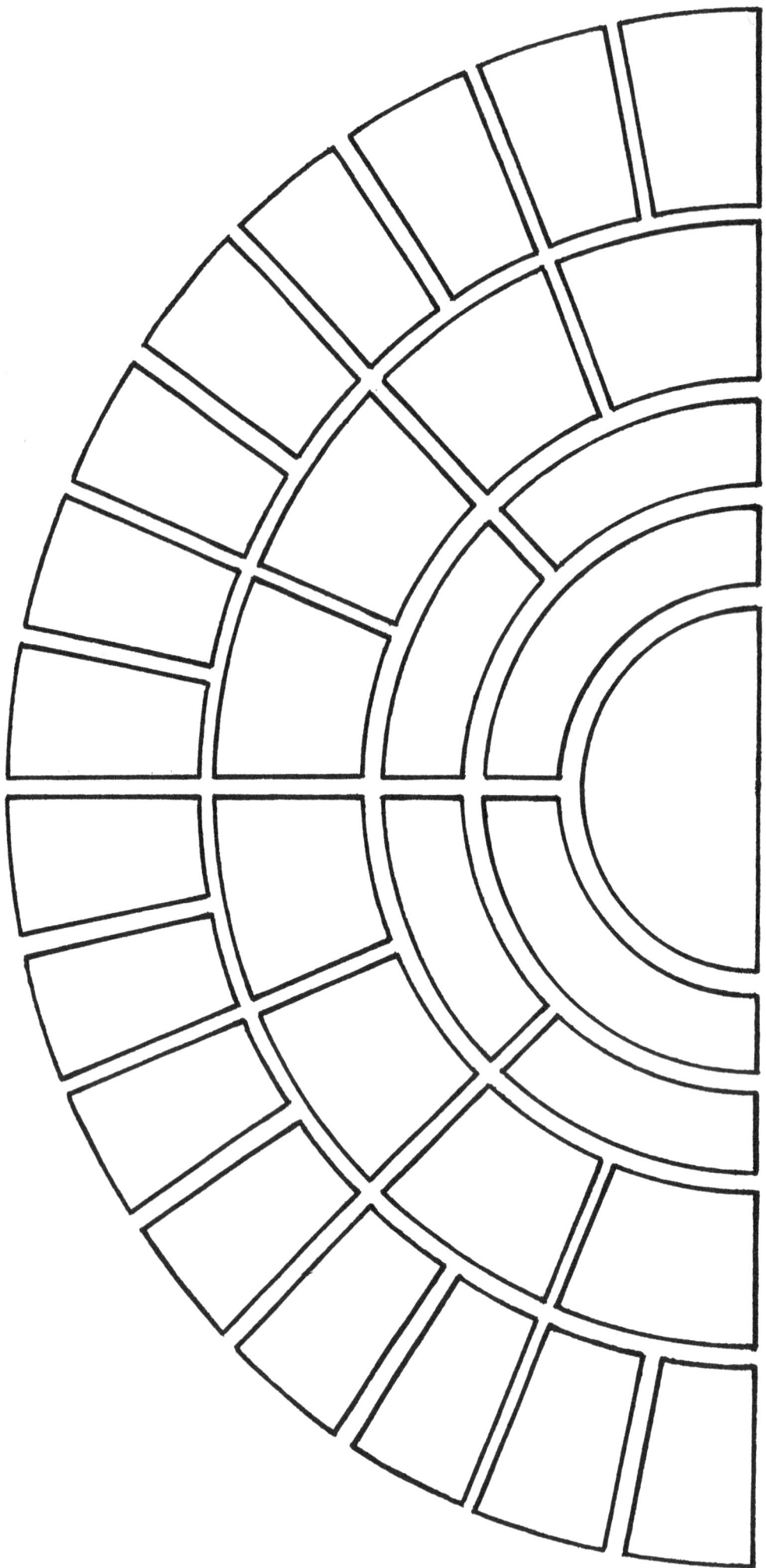

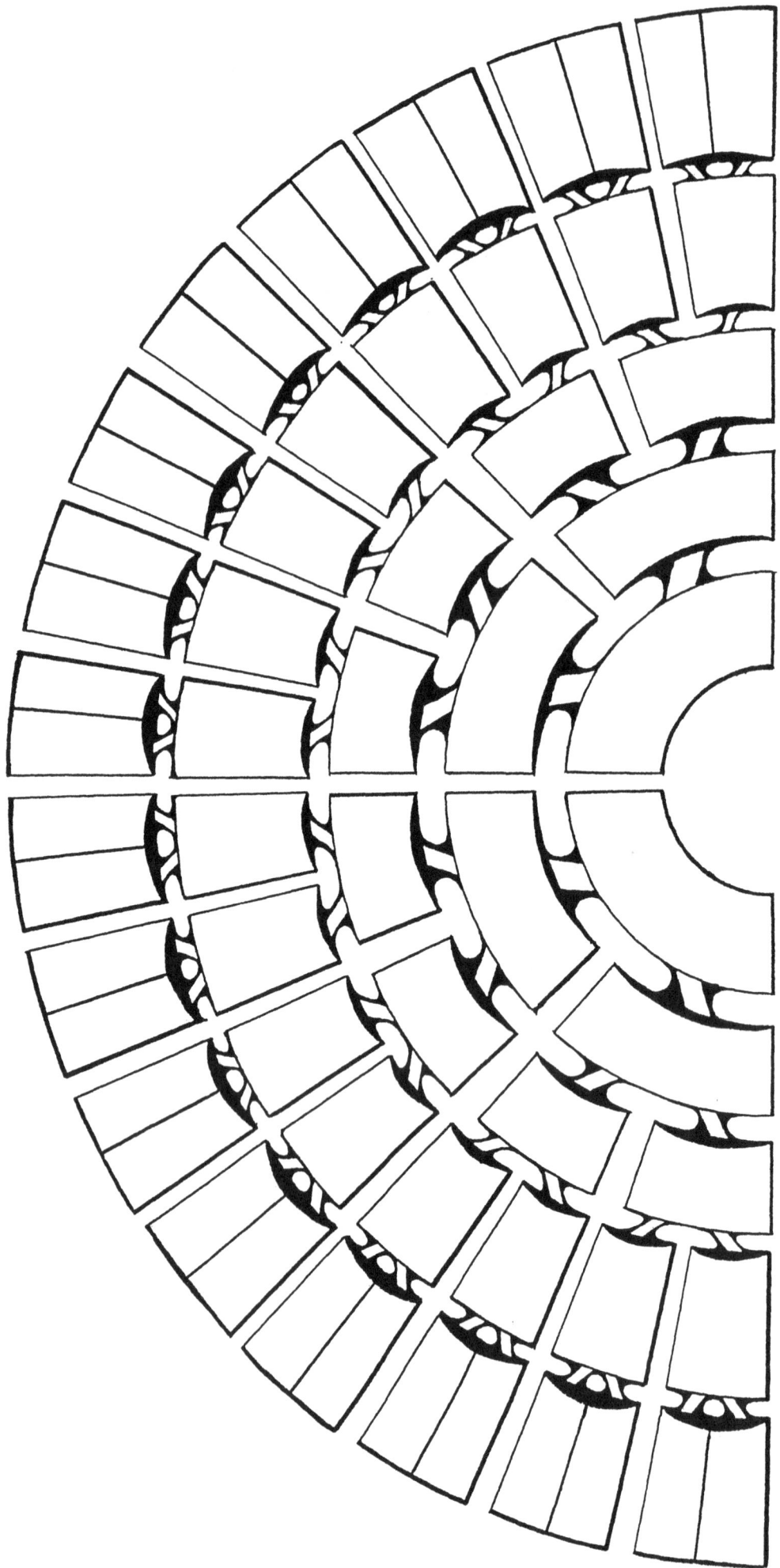

YOUR TURN......

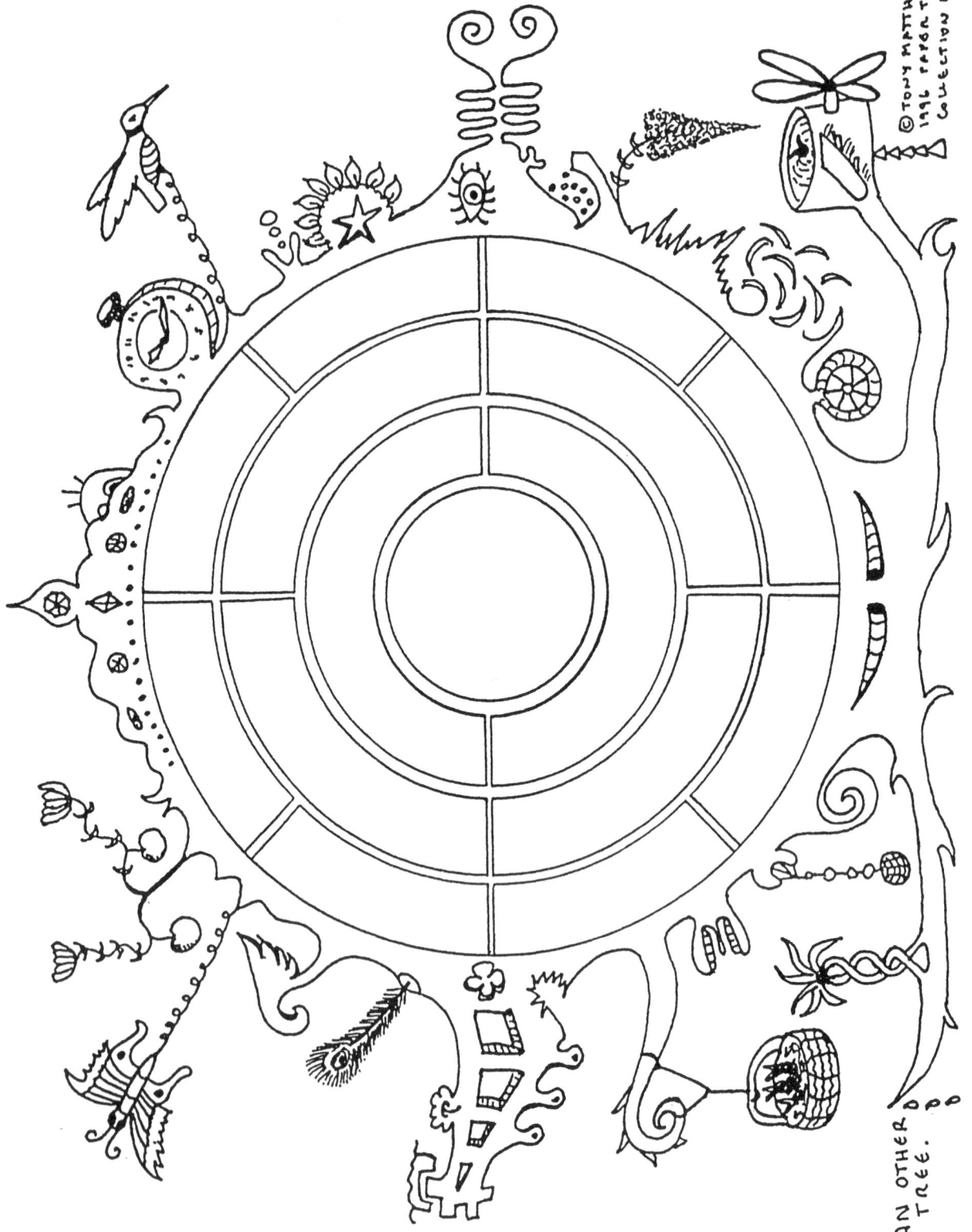

AN OTHER
TREE.

THE MATHS

You will need pencil, ruler, compass, and a right-angle (even a hardback book cover will do, a box..... Right, draw a horizontal line, then a vertical one up from the middle (we're doing semi-circular). Next draw arcs on your baseline. You'll need one for each generation, and one extra, plus double up if you are doing boxes with spaces between them.. Now we do the radials. It is possible to use a protractor, but you get into fractions of arcs. I simply measure from where the arc meets the baseline to where it meets the vertical. Mark a spot half way along, and run your next radial from this to the centre. This first one (and repeat other side of vertical) gives you a 45' radial.

Repeat measuring from where your new radial meets the arc, along to the baseline. Mark the halfway point, draw next radial to centre. This will be at 22and1/2 '. Repeat other side of first radial to upright, and 2 more other side of upright.

Curved boxes should be appearing, and you will eventually rub out parts of your construction lines to leave one box as the base arch (for you), 2 boxes in the next arch for your parents, 4 in the next for grandparents, and so on. You can go as far as you like, but look at the boxes being formed......you have to be able to write names in them, so you may have to draw an arc further out to get a longer box.

Continue dividing the outer boxes as neccesary, by finding the halfway point between where two adjacent radials meet an arc, then draw in the new radial from this point to the centre where your baseline and upright meet. It sounds complicated, but is simple mathematics, oft repeated, and you'll soon get into a rythym. By the time you get to do 64 boxes for your great great great great grandparents you will be an expert (or have developed a squint !)

I found that 8 generations is the most that I could comfortably fit onto an 18X24 sheet.......but using a nail, string and pencil for the arcs, you could cover a whole wall. You will probably have longer and shorter branches to fill in, we all do (that Irish grandmother in London still eludes me), but remember what a treasure your Tree will be to your descendants. There will be reason why you can't trace one line so far back, and that reason is part of your family story too. Maybe a descendant will be inspired to try and fill in the blanks.

RESEARCH

Even a simple 5 generation Tree, yourself and 30 ancestors, is really a substantial frame for others to either find all the siblings, aunts, cousins, and in-laws from, or to tie your Tree in with theirs......
5 generations can span 150 years. Birth, and marriage, date and place are the vital pieces of information......siblings will often be found in birth, church or census records : find John in Austin Texas in 1880, look a few years either side for siblings, or find the whole bunch in the census, you know from your Tree who the parents are. Then find those parents' siblings, or John's children's or wife's siblings.....each time the starting point is on the Tree. Of course, if those shoe boxes under the bed survive too, then the job is already done. Your Tree is the skeleton, but the stories, photos and all are the flesh, so try to copy, share and preserve them too.

You can draw a Tree with everyone on it, in the traditional way, but even here you can use clip art, stencils etc., etc., to decorate it. Again, a simple border will work perfectly, but you could also add pictures with the names.........a hammer for grandpa who was a carpenter, a ship for Willy who ran away to sea, a saucepan for mum who was a great cook, a heart for your dear wife, and so on. It's fun, and it's informative.
What little picture would you put for yourself ?

Research is not just about the names and dates. You need to bring these folk to life. Basic facts can be gleaned from such as Church Records and Census, but there is much else to discover along the way. The Tax records tell you how rich or poor they were (or claimed to be !). Land Records put them into a place, and you might discover what crops they grew; who their neighbours were (the girl next door, that the son married, and her parents, perhaps all part of a group that had emigrated there together ?); then the County History might mention them, or events that they might have been involved in; Court Records could throw up a surprise or two; Military Records detail an important part of someone's life; Newspapers are a wonderful source of background, as well as specific, information; general History provides a framework for your family, and often explains why, for example, they moved; old job descriptions illuminate; Wills fascinate; and a figure slowly emerges.

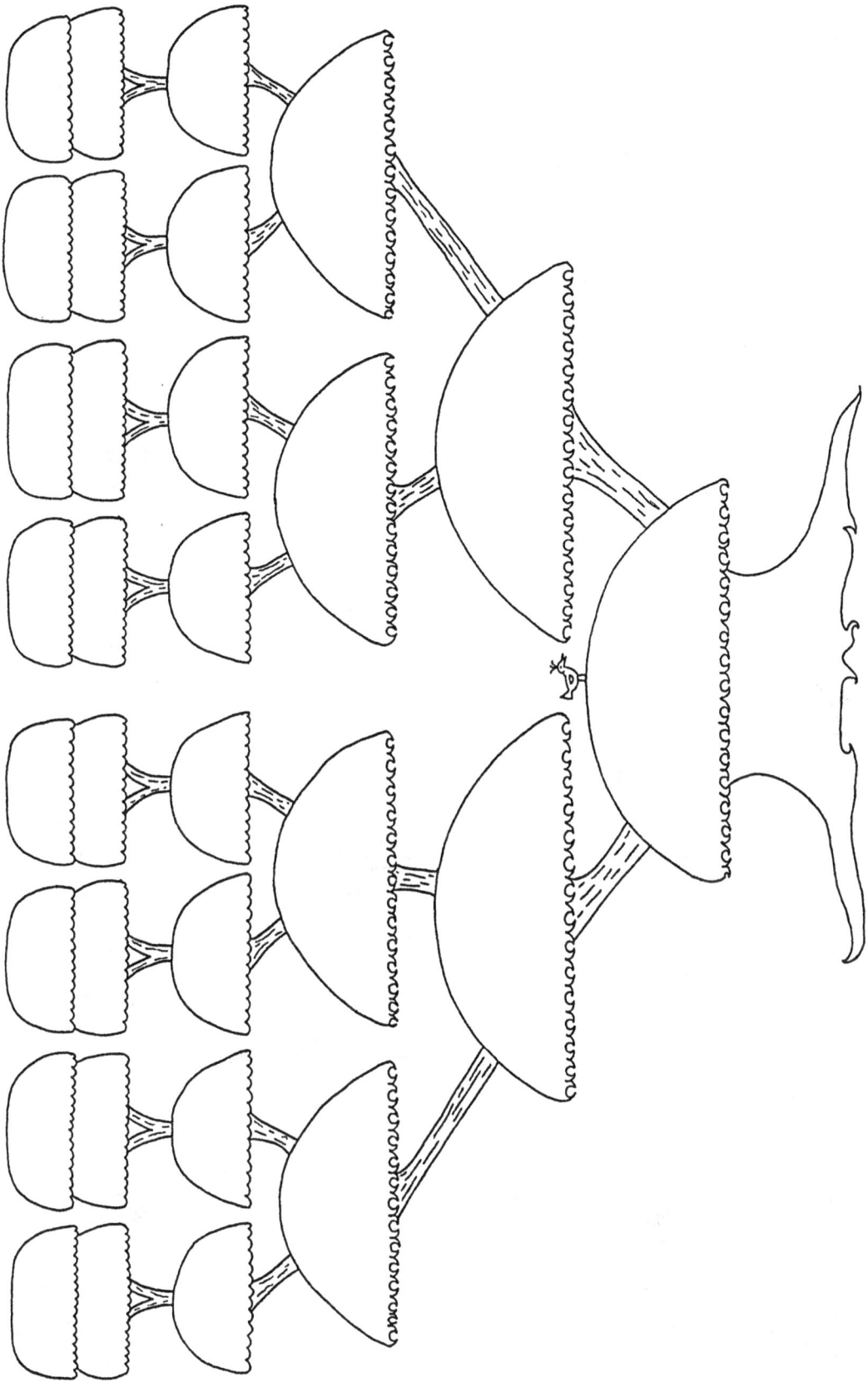

THE CHESTNUTS

8. Father's Father's Father

9. Father's Father's Mother

10. Father's Mother's Father

11. Father's Mother's Mother

12. Mother's Father's Father

13. Mother's Father's Mother

14. Mother's Mother's Father

15. Mother's Mother's Mother

4. FATHER'S FATHER

5. FATHER'S MOTHER

6. MOTHER'S FATHER

7. MOTHER'S MOTHER

2. FATHER

3. MOTHER

1. SELF

Remember to leave your own file behind : your details and documentation; photos and certificates; major facts of your life; a description of your character (try to be fairly truthful !); your job, likes and dislikes, politics and religion, etc., etc.

Dig out all that you already know about your family : bible, documents, diaries, letters. obituaries and so on.

Then grill your granny, and every family member, friends, neighbours and workmates, to get both the maximum information about your ancestors, and differing views of their character and activities. You want names, dates, places, photo or description, character, humour, career, hobbies, achievements, artifacts, life events, connection to local and world events........it's ok to be nosey ! You never know from where, or who, a vital clue may come. Most family legends are doubtful, but hold a germ of truth.

Then you can turn to your local Library, Genealogical Society, and branch of the LDS (Mormon/Jesus Christ Church Of Latter Day Saints), plus the Web and Internet. Double check all information with original records : any index, transcription, computer list, family history etc. is open to human mistakes......even the original records such as the Census and Church Registers can be flawed.

You would be wise to get a beginner's guide, or take a course at a Genealogical Society. Talk to folk, ask questions, listen to the answers. Your family history research will be fun and addictive, but needs to be done properly too, for your own sake as well as your descendants'.

Find out how to preserve your findings.

Copy and share the important stuff with at least one other person.

Get organised. Once the first pile of papers falls off the kitchen table this warning won't be neccesary. Aim for files that a 10 year old could decipher.

Assume everything that you have found is wrong, then try and prove that it is. Anything that passes is elevated to "possible". Try to get 2 or more different records for the same fact. This may all sound a bit heavy, but you are recreating history, your family history, to pass on, so it needs to be right. Then you get the warm glow of a job well done, and the thanks of present and future family.

Along the way you will have uncovered many amazing things, met interesting people, and, more importantly, learnt much about yourself.

WRITABLE SHAPES

Straight boxes, fan shapes, spaces in between.......after dozens of designs in these styles I came to yet another breakthrough. Once you tune into these new ways of looking at "Trees" yourself, you will quickly realize the endless possibilities that are opened up.

I got fed up doing boxes.

Suddenly whole new vistas opened before me. All that we really need in a Tree are spaces to write the names........any shaped space that provides room to write on is perfectly good.

My first attempt was a half step.....I did trucks, which broke the mould, even though they still have a certain boxlike quality. But move on from there......know a youngster into dinosaurs ? How about using the outline of 1 Tyrannosaurus Rex, 2 Triceratops, then 4 Brontosaurus, and so on. Maybe you could cut out the shapes and paste them onto a picture/poster/wallpaper that shows a jungle. One neat Tree.

There are sensible possibilities too, but I find the humourous ones spark of more ideas, so........know a plumber ? 1 washing machine, 2 bath tubs, 4 sinks.....and a maze of pipes in the background, or the pipes as trunk and branches, with sinks and tubs dangling from them........ The whole point is to find a theme that is particular to the person or family, to tell about them, and create something unique.

Stencils and stickers could be used to create a night sky (on blue paper) with small planets, comets, moon, rocket, and large stars to write the names on.

So many ideas spring to mind, so many subjects, hobbies, careers, all with a "writable" shape that you could use. Silhouettes are a simple choice to make an appropriate shape. If you find a good picture as clip-art, you can white-out the centre to provide writing space. Once any shape is duplicated, and put into a pattern, it becomes more significant and artistic. I once saw whole pictures made up of identical postcards that had been glued partly on top of each other, like a fanned deck of playing cards.

Nor do the shapes have to be in isolation......how about a vase of flowers, with a name written in the centre of each one ?

Smaller pictures, or an appropriate background would be good, and a border could add to it all.

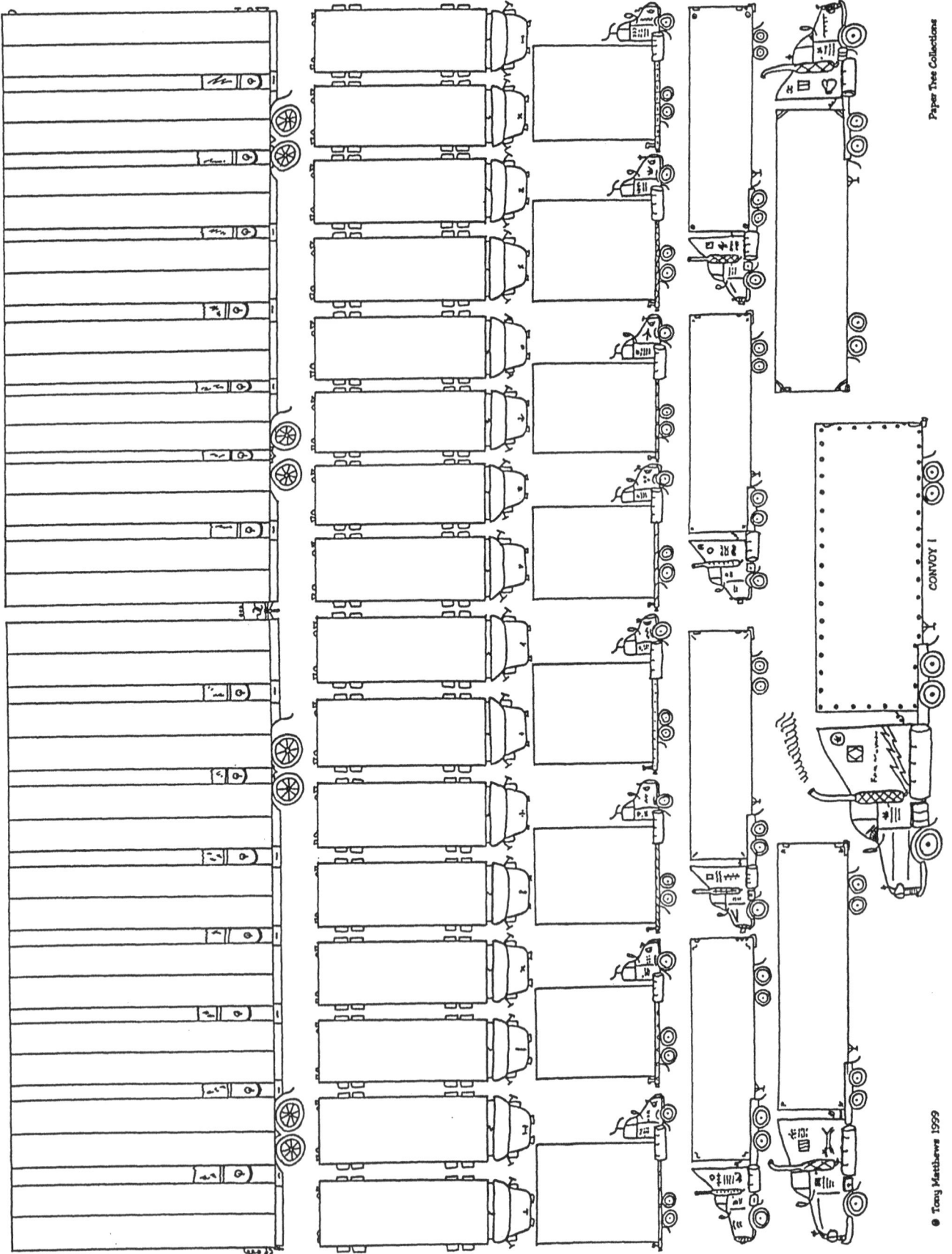

CONVOY I

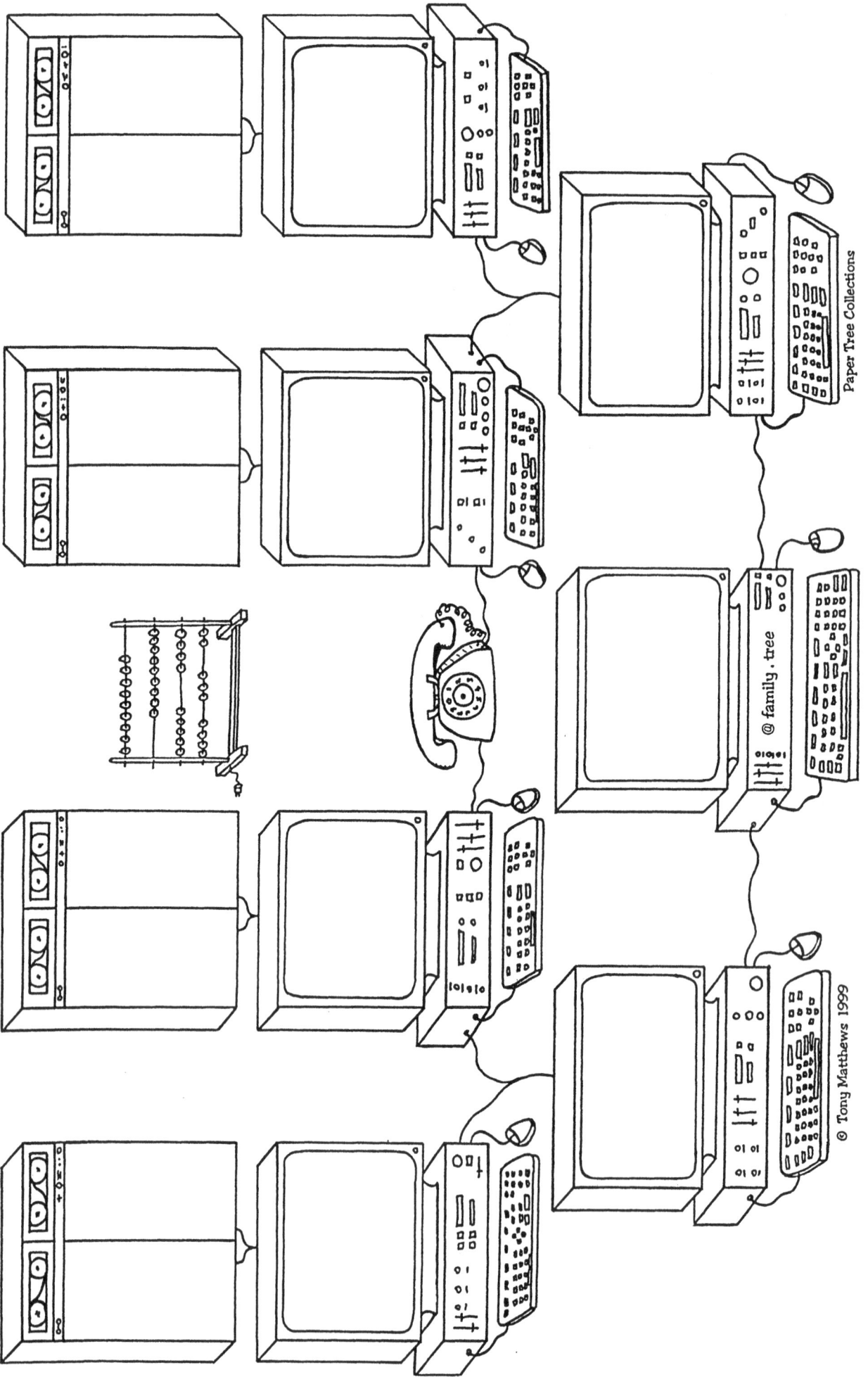

Paper Tree Collections

@ family . tree

© Tony Matthews 1999

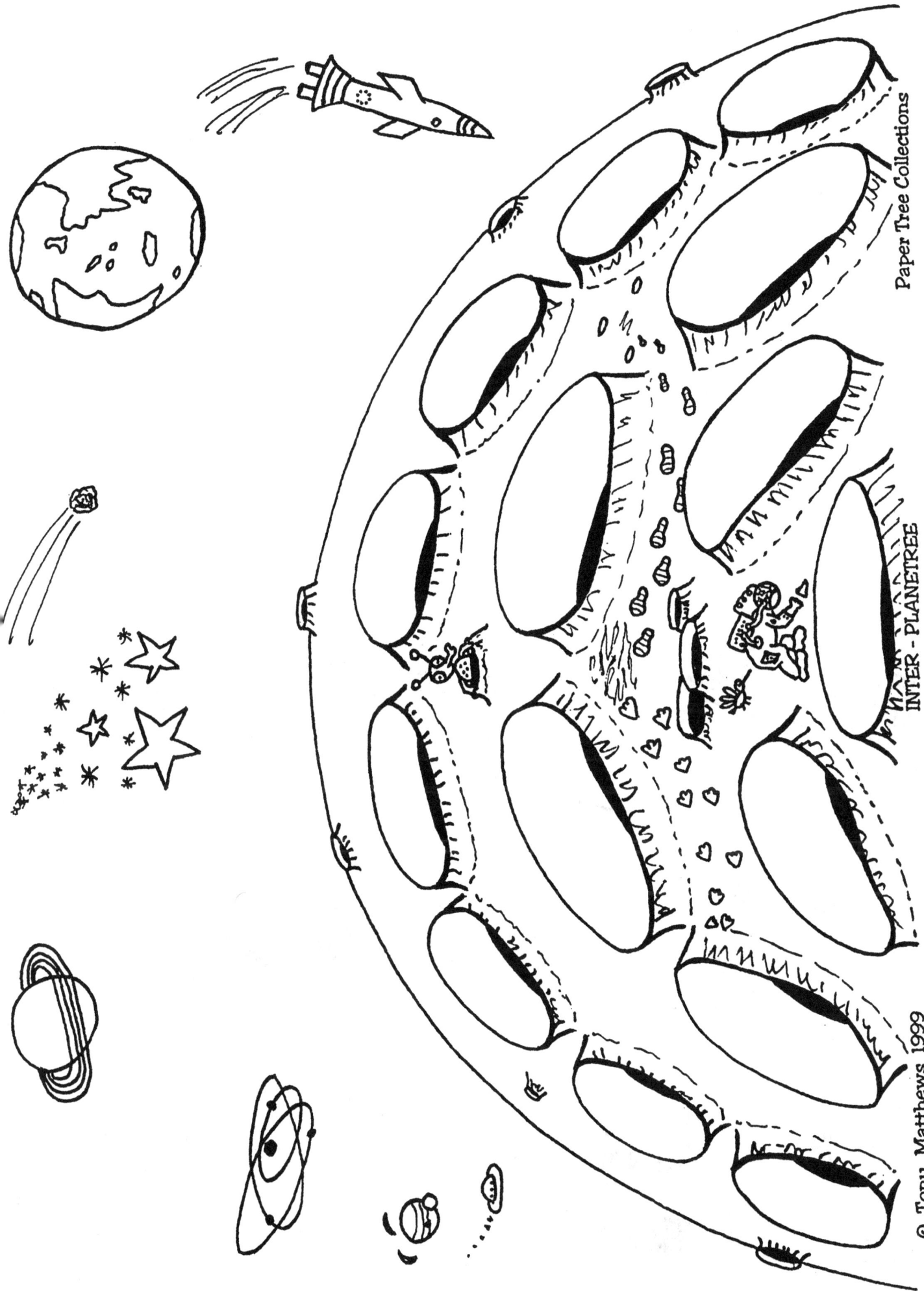

INTER - PLANETREE

OUR TREK © Tony Matthews 2000

NUMBER PILES

But if you can't think of a writable shape ?........then we come to the pile. All you need is enough space to write the number (room for the person's initials too would provide a good double check). Then you just write the name on a grid below.....particularly easy for the cut'n'paste of computerised/typewriter names. This style is also great for making cards, with the numbered picture on the front, your message in the middle, and the grid of names on the back so that it can be seen beside the picture when the card is opened out. Cards are great for asking cousins questions, sharing family information, even requests to Archives would be more noticed on a card than just a letter. If you do your cards on regular cardstock, they will still go through a computer printer to add your message.

You can stack any pictures, stencil shapes, clip art, etc., on plain paper, or with a fancy poster/wallpaper/wrapping paper background. You could use the fan or square shapes just with numbers in. Again, you could always add a border.

The possibilities really are endless, from hearts to tractors to ships to pigs to quilts to candy to toys to to to.

An interesting point on mathematical beauty. When numbering these ancestors you'll find that they conform to a simple rule : the father is always twice the child, and mother follows dutifully after. Try it out......parents of 3 are 6 and 7, parents of 7 are 14 and 15, parents of 24 are 48 and 49. Traditionally the father always comes first, and goes to the left, or above.

Many of the ideas that I have mentioned will work on several of the different styles, you can mix and match, you can even use a traditional picture of a tree.....but instead of squares, why not use the shapes of birds as your writable spaces, or number spaces ? Maybe kites or kittens get stuck in the tree, or UFO's land there ? Even just a tree will work, I did a willow tree, with side branches to form box-like spaces, all in a fan shape. Turn that shape upside down.....could it be antlers, a candleabra, a bowl of fruit......? Now turn it sideways..........

OTHER TREES

You can even get fancier. Genealogists enjoy puzzles, so I've tried out mazes, spirals, and more. How about a box of cookies, with 1 round one, 2 square, 4 triangular, 8 oval........ Once, I even went back to actual boxes, but added cartoons of people being people. At present (Nov. 1999) I am working on a design that will have "writable shapes", in the standard 1, 2, 4, 8 etc., format, but the shapes won't be the same.....the whole will be a cohesive picture though......the "2" may be a unicorn and a dragon. The "4" may be a tree, a mountain, a castle, and a cloud, or perhaps a knight, fairy, wizard and elf, but done as a number pile. I will try and write a genealogical poem to go with it, that incorporates the figures and features. The revolution is far from over, and you are welcome to join in. I know there are some great Tree ideas out there.

What I have tried to do is to break away from traditional styles by exploring virgin territory, but also by adapting recognisable constructions. Plus, I have tried to add new elements of fun, colour and imagination that refresh the whole concept, and maybe encourage more folk to have a go. I've had fun, and there is enjoyment and achievement in doing a Tree, of course, but, if you will pardon the pun, at the root of it all is the same old pedigree chart, or fan, and the means of organising and preserving family information to pass on as an heirloom.

This is more important now than ever. At one time families stayed for generations in and around the same location, and thus were relatively (and there's more puns to come) easy to trace. Nowadays families are branching out all over the world, which leaves a much harder trail to follow. Even records are being kept differently : paper has actually proved to be quite durable over the centuries, but do you know just how brief the life of a cd is by comparison? So, this is a good time to be gathering your folks together, before some records are lost forever......or until a Time Machine is invented.

Anyway, I hope that I have planted some seeds and inspired you to have a go, you have nothing to lose, and much to gain.

I can think of dozens of Trees that I don't have the time (or sometimes the expertise) to do, but the Tree that you create yourself will be more important and satisfying to you, and valued by your current family, and descendants.

I look forward to seeing them.

Tony

1.

2.

3.

4.

5.

6.

7.

8.

9.

10.

11.

12.

13.

14.

15.

"GREETINGS."

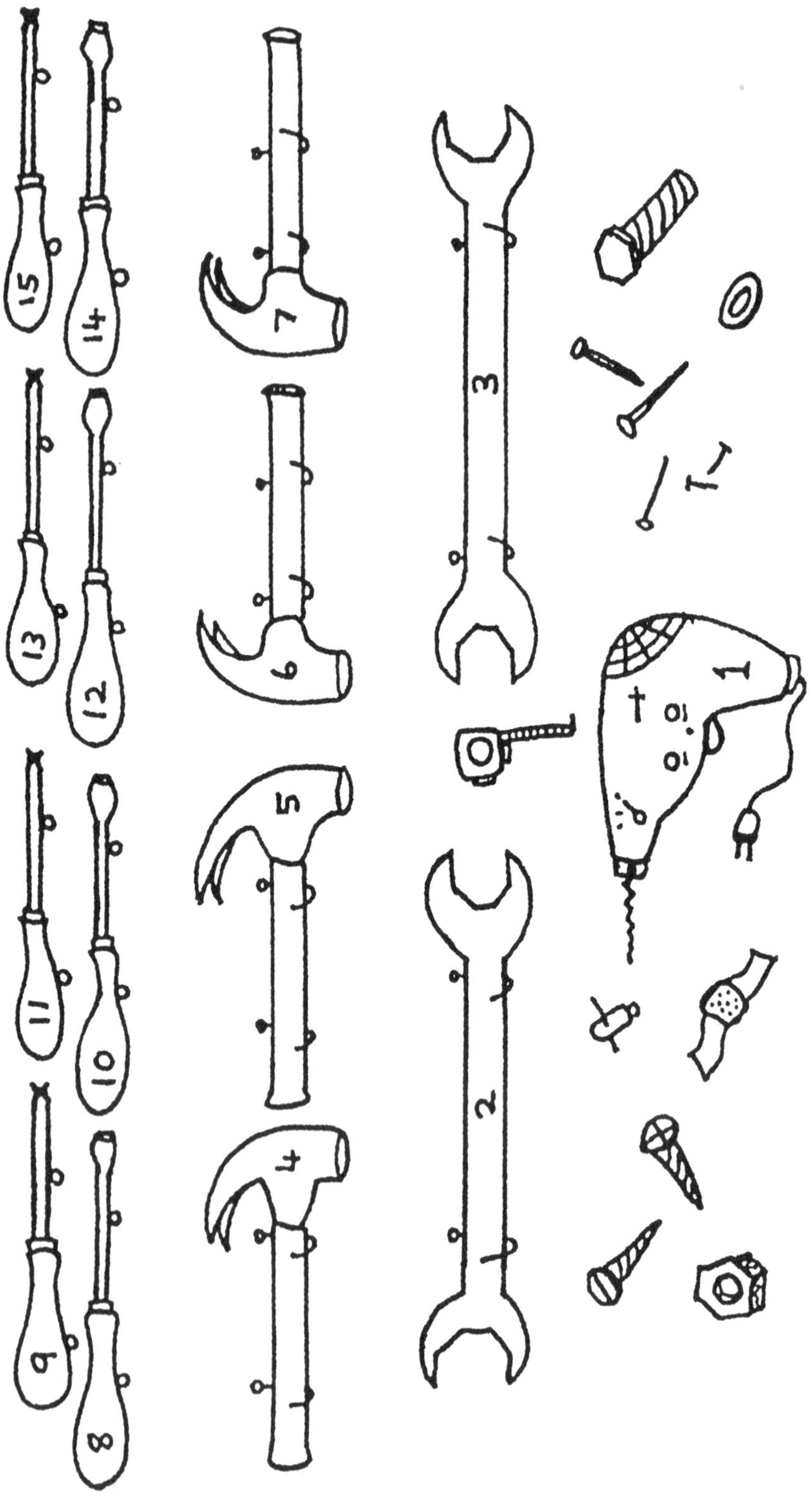
1
2
3
4
5
6
7
8
9
10
11
12
13
14
15

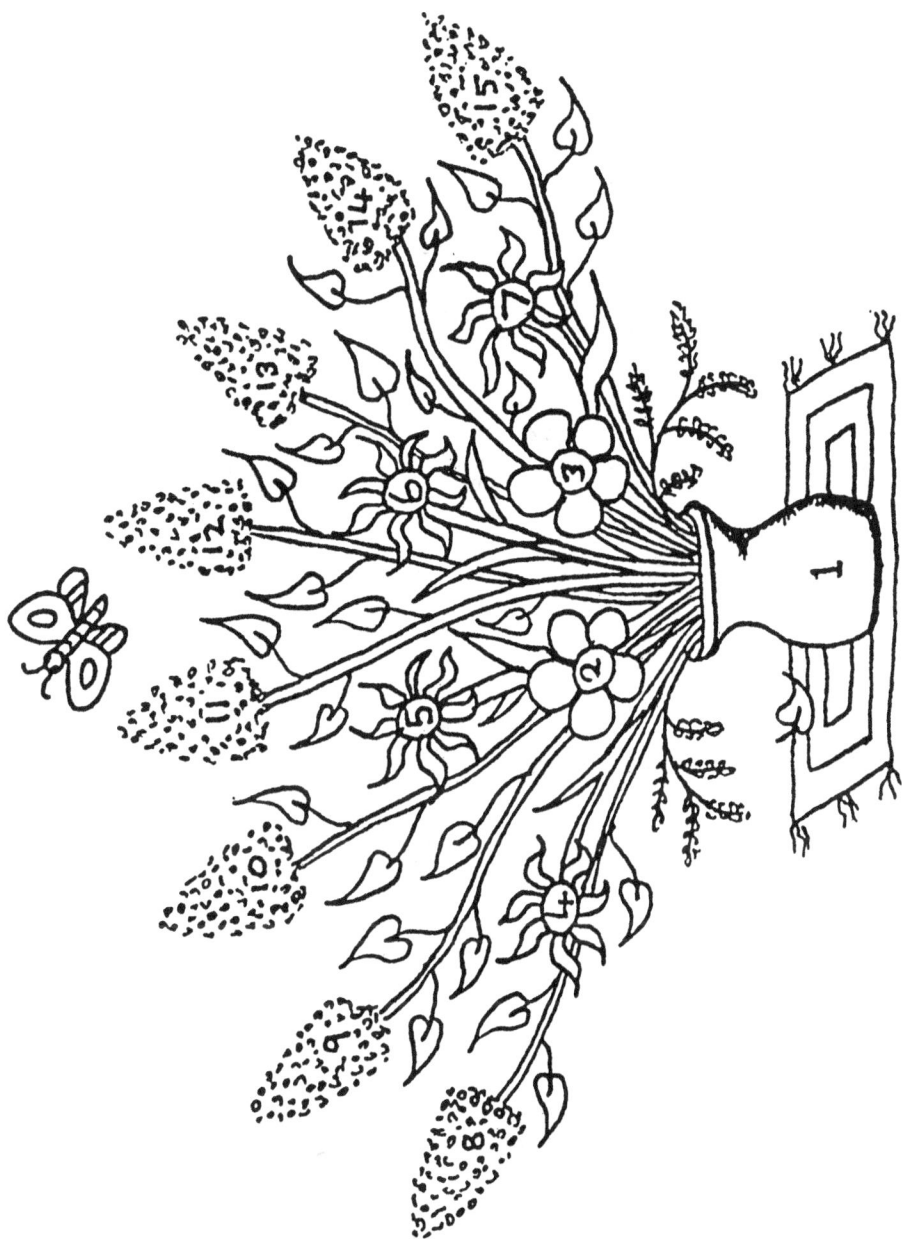

NEW HOME....

....OLD FAMILY.

1 ....

2 ....

3 ....

4 ....

5 ....

6 ....

7 ....

8 ....

9 ....

10 ....

11 ....

12 ....

13 ....

14 ....

15 ....

1 ....

2 ....

3 ....

4 ....

5 ....

6 ....

7 ....

8 ....

9 ....

10 ....

11 ....

12 ....

13 ....

14 ....

15 ....

16 ....

17 ....

18 ....

19 ....

20 ....

21 ....

22 ....

23 ....

24 ....

25 ....

26 ....

27 ....

28 ....

29 ....

30 ....

31 ....

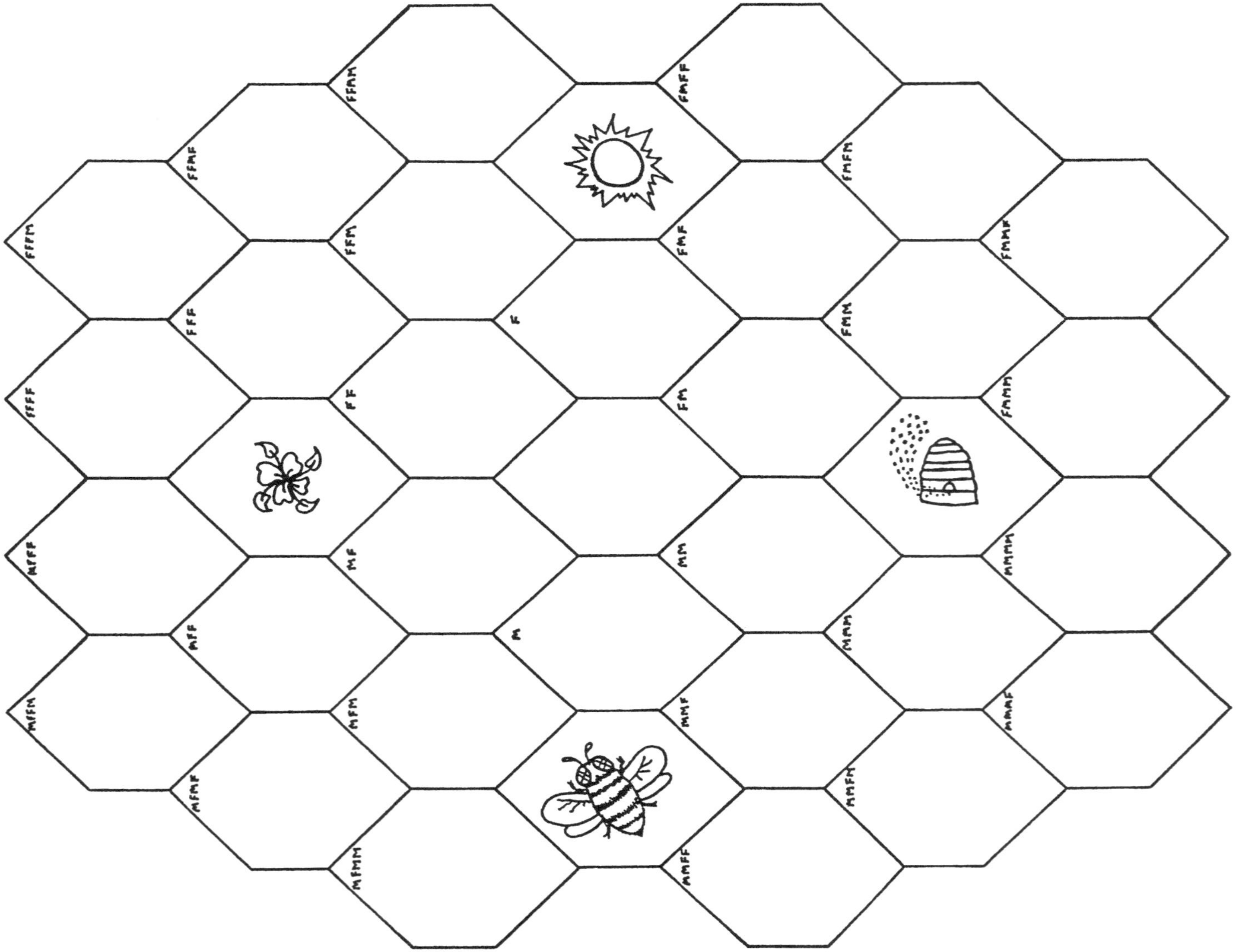

Paper Tree Collections

MFFM   MFFF   FFFF   FFFM

MFMF   MFF   FFF   FFMF

MFMM   MFM   MF   FF   FFM   FFMM

M   F

MMFF   MMF   MM   FM   FMF   FMFF

MMFM   MMM   FMM   FMFM

MMMF   MMMM   FMMM   FMMF

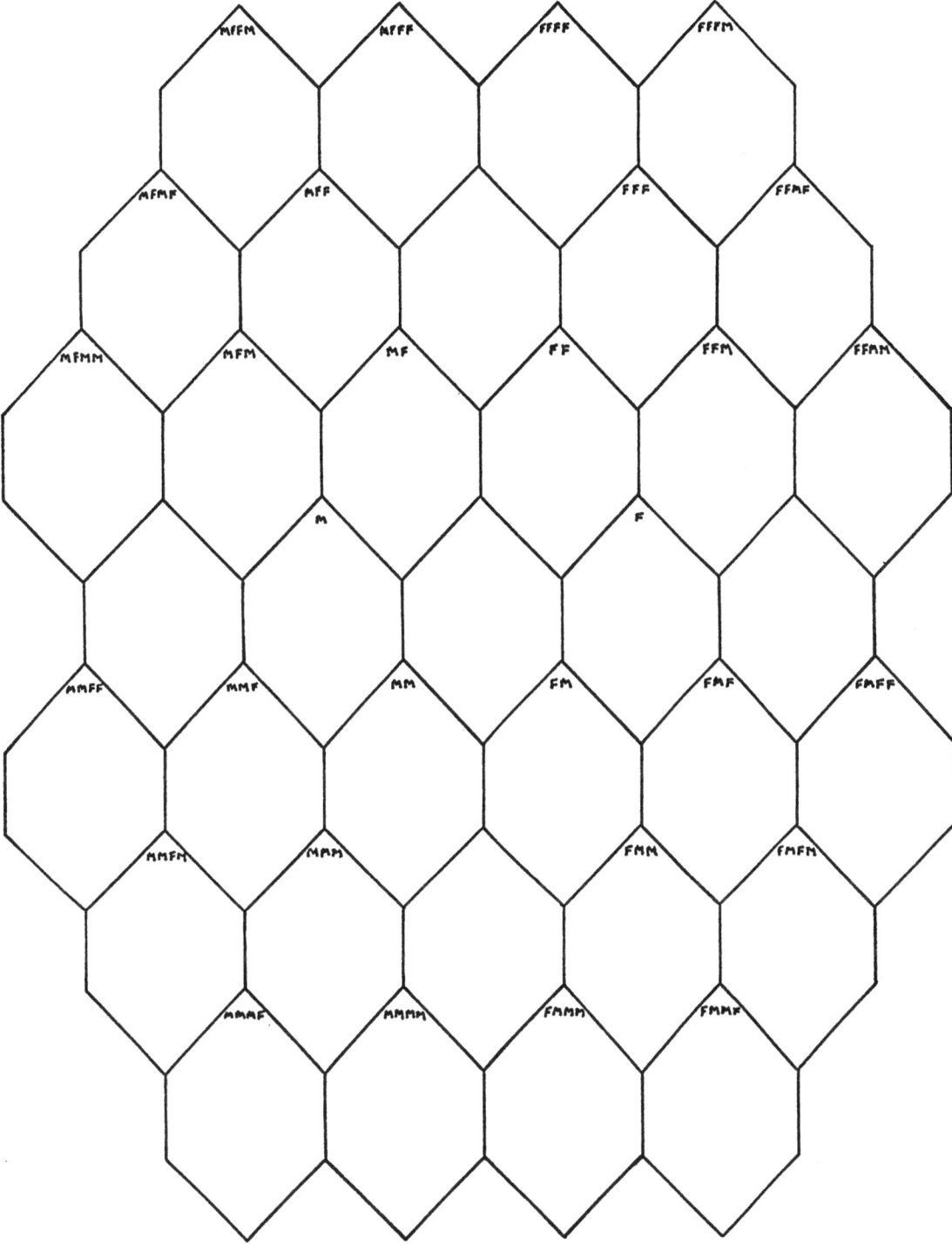

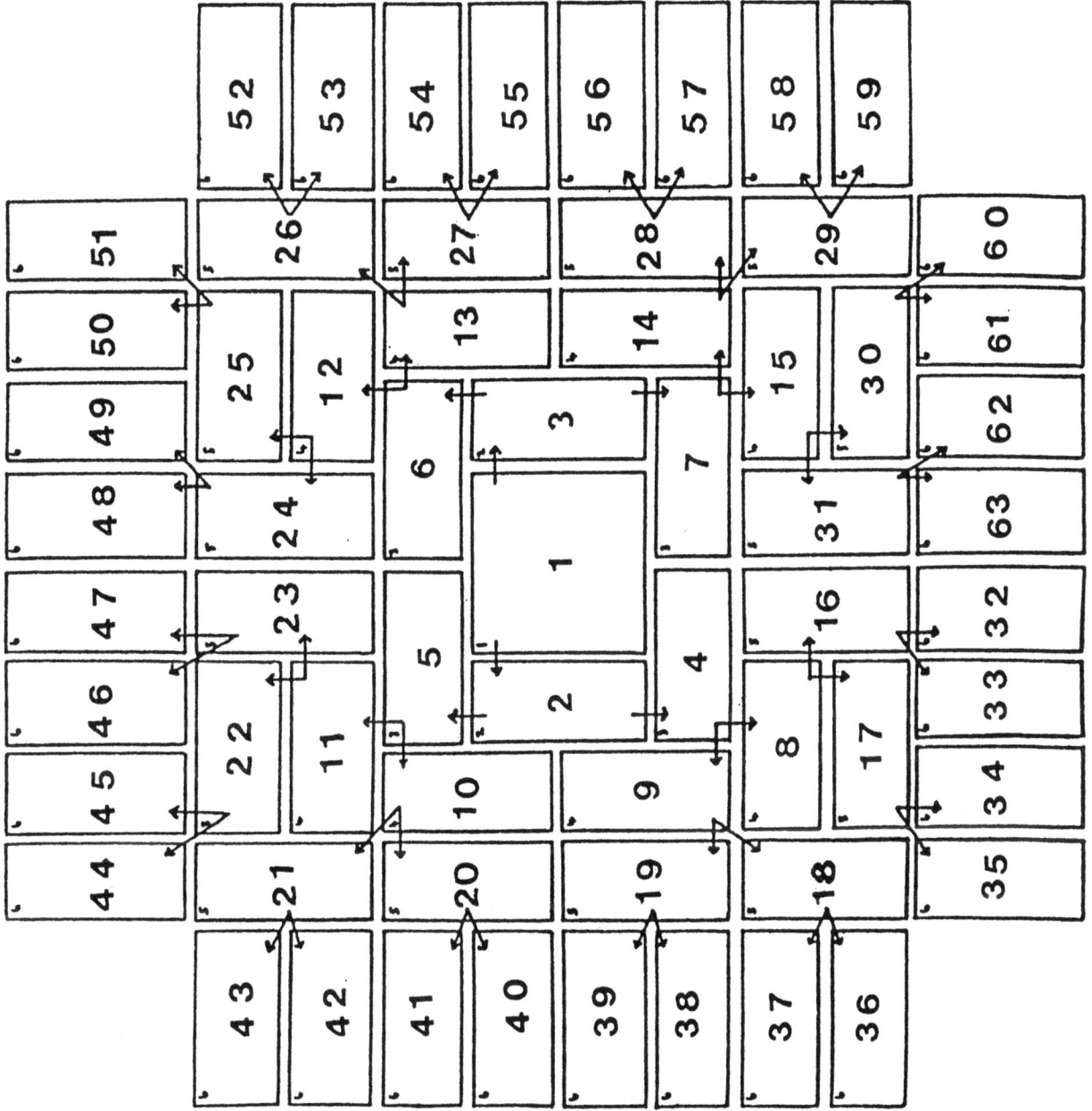

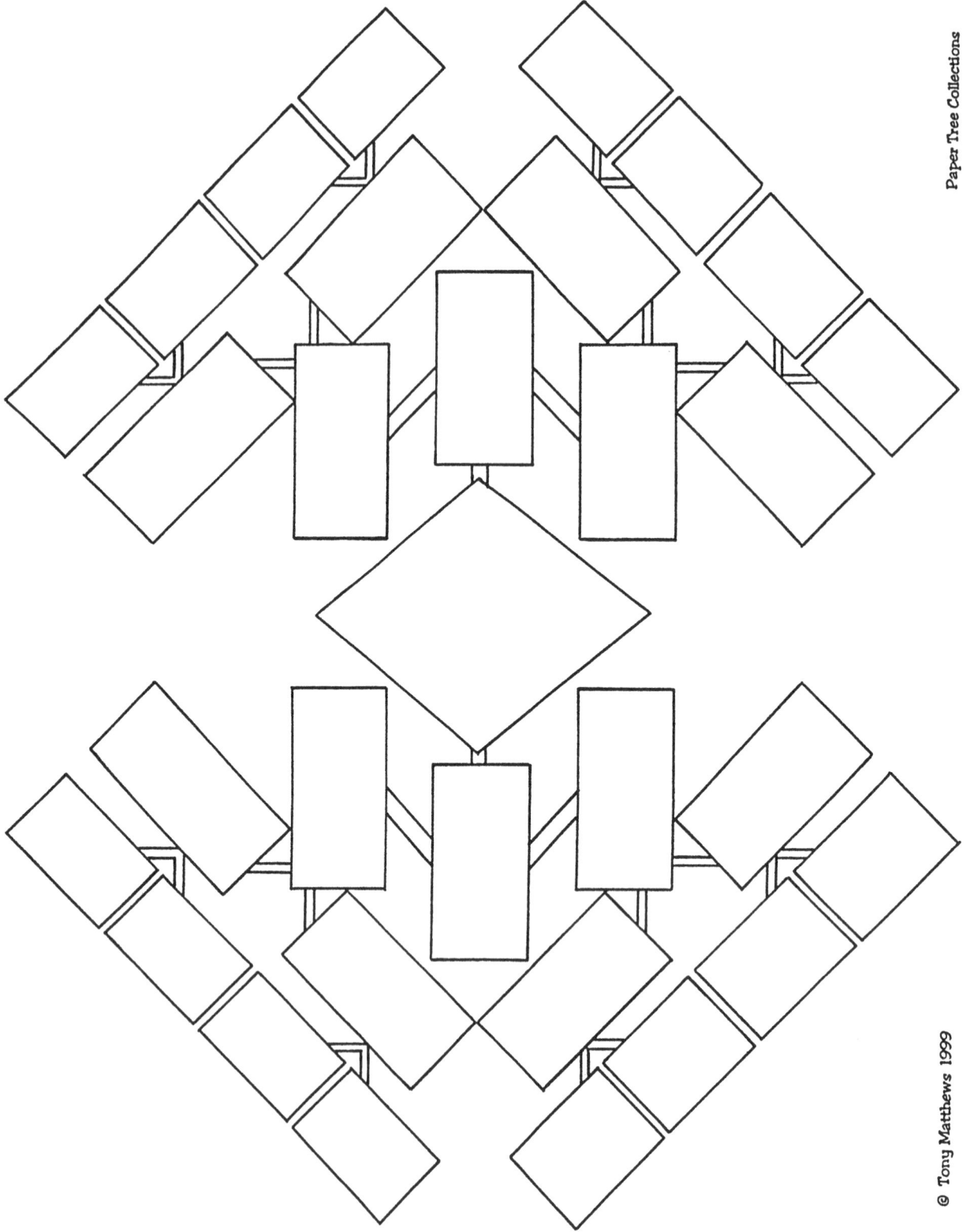

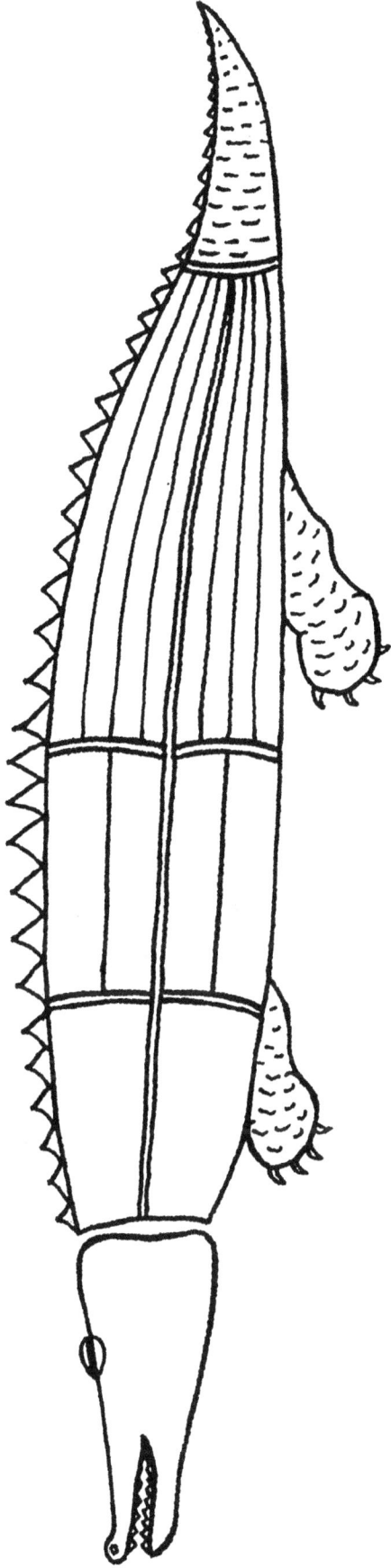

© Tony Matthews 1999

OLD CROCS

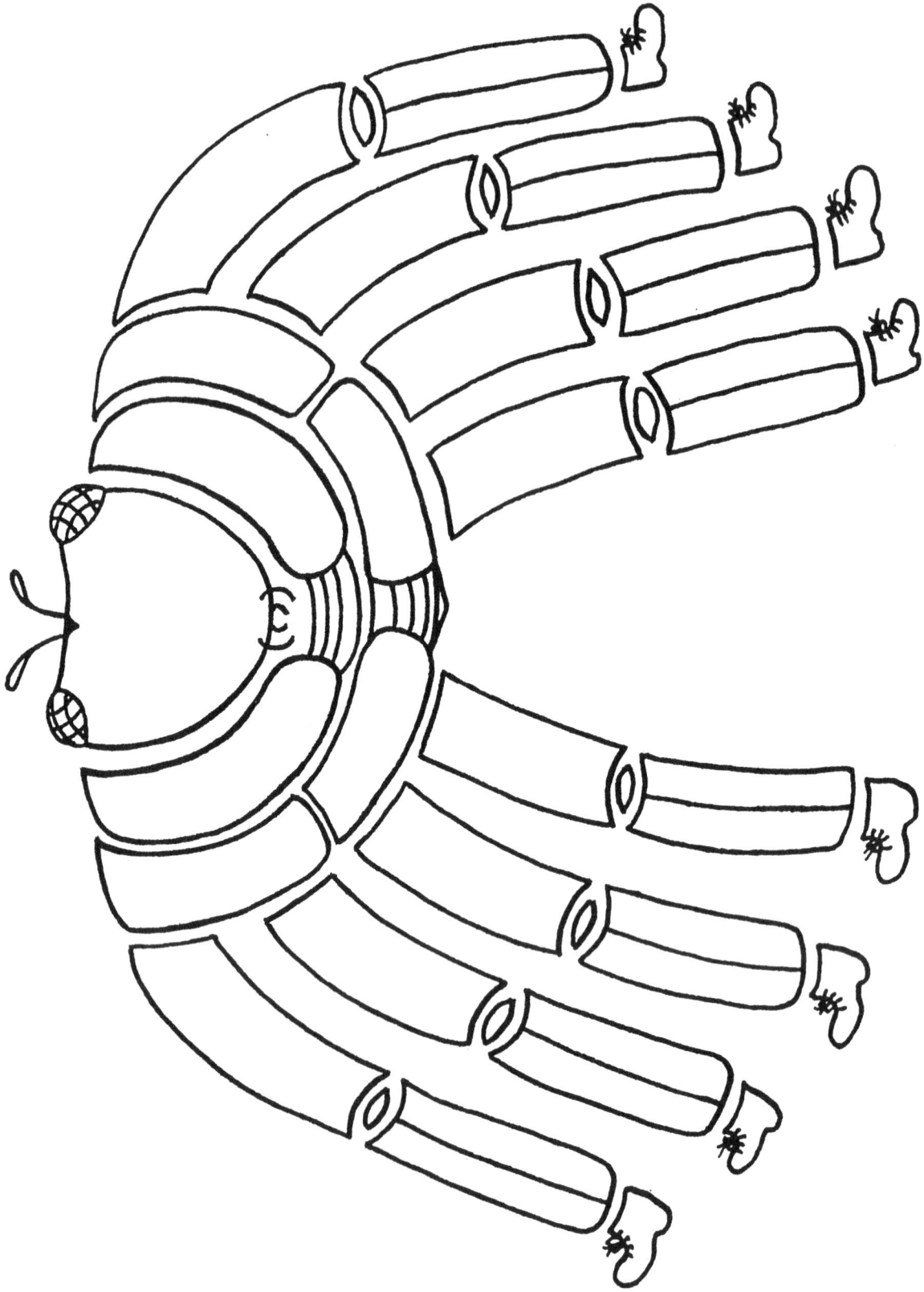

MY FAMILY (BUGS ME)

© Tony Matthews 1999

TAPESTRY

Some, from the forests they came,
And some sailed across the Seas.
Over mountains, some made their way,
And some from castles, some from fields.

Elf maiden and warrior bold,
Wizards, servants, queens,
Farmers, merchants, poor untold,
Priests, sinners, pioneers.

From all corners of this quilted land,
And all walks of life, journeying on.
Strong or weak, their roads they trod,
Happy or grim, all joining hands.

From their bodies, we all came,
From their hearts, our hearts beat,
From their thoughts, our minds aflame,
Our hands join, it is complete.

Across the years a web is grown,
Generations weave a tapestry.
We, the warp and weft, woven
On a loom Time cannot stay.

Though threads be lost or broken,
And colours dim and fade....
Yet the visions swells again
As our children laugh and play.

****

© Tony Matthews 1999

© Tony Matthews 2001

WHAT-A-FAMILY !

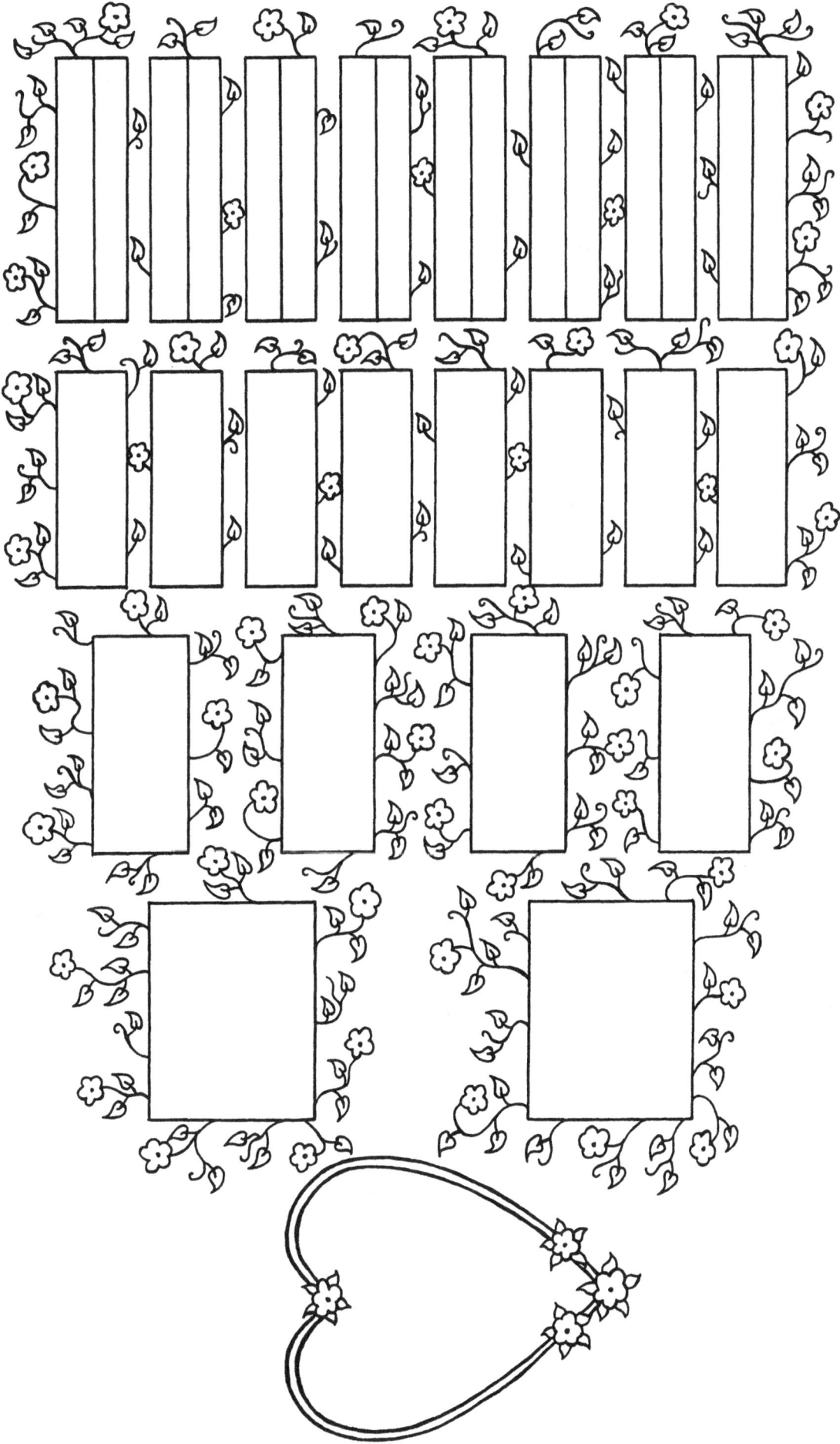

You move through Time
Like a ship at sea,
Sails full blowing
Wild and free.

Turning to the currents,
Answering the wind,
Tugging at your anchor
For you won't be pinned.

Around the globe in majesty,
Your pennants telling tales
Of long lost lands and people,
And adventures flung on gales.

And Centuries you overturned
Like pebbles on a beach,
And Mysteries like crabs
That scuttled out of reach.

And aeons like oceans
That you sail to explore,
And History like landmarks,
The Dead piled on the shore.

And Futures in the sunset,
Glowing red on your prow,
As you head into Time's tide
On the tidal wave called Now.

And all Men could be sailors,
Pearls of Wisdom the prize,
Yet we paddle on the shoreline
......And are proud of our lives.

****
"Ahoy, Kinship" : words and image
© Tony Matthews 2001
A Paper Tree production.

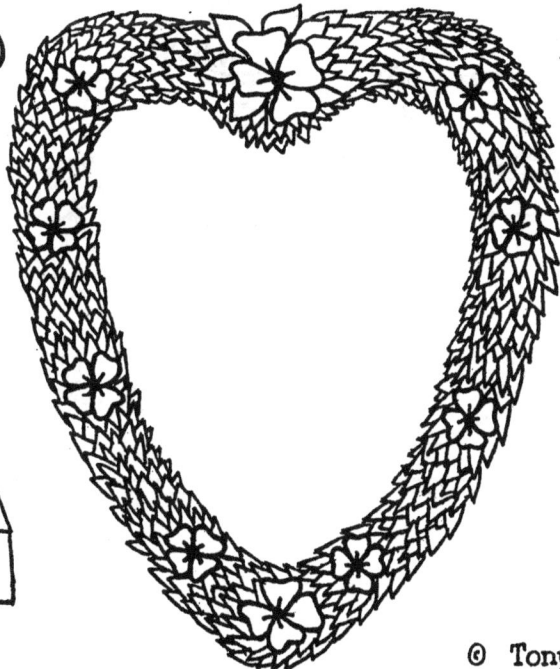
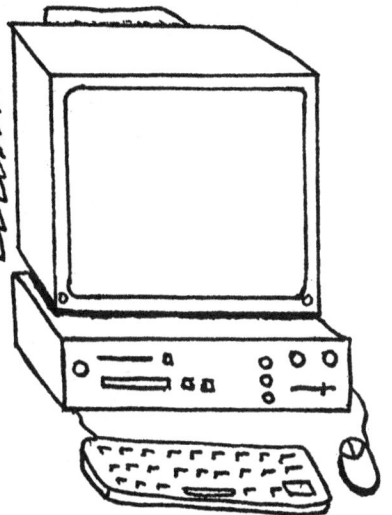

© Tony Matthews 2000

FOR OUR CHILDREN

© Tony Matthews 1999

P.S. Yes, it's a "Tree" too !

www.ingramcontent.com/pod-product-compliance
Lightning Source LLC
Chambersburg PA
CBHW081203270326
41930CB00014B/3277